# BUDGETMAKING
A Workbook of Public Budgeting Theory and Practice

# BUDGETMAKING

## A Workbook of Public Budgeting Theory and Practice

EDWARD A. LEHAN

ST. MARTIN'S PRESS | NEW YORK

Copyright © 1984 by St. Martin's Press, Inc.
All Rights Reserved.
Manufactured in the United States of America.
8 7 6 5 4
fedcba
For information, write St. Martin's Press, Inc.,
175 Fifth Avenue, New York, N.Y. 10010

cover design: Darby Downey
text design: Leon Bolognese
ISBN: 0-312-10755-2

*Acknowledgment*
The budget formulation guidelines on pp. 73–78 incorporate material appearing in Edward A. Lehan, *Simplified Governmental Budgeting* (Chicago: Municipal Finance Officers Association, 1981), pp. 40–45. Reprinted with permission.

# CONTENTS

*A Note to Teachers and Students*   ix

**Benchmark Essay**   1
Clarify Your Thinking   *1*

**UNIT 1: What Is Good Budgeting?**   5
Not an Easy Question   *5*
Another Chance   *6*
Looking for Fundamentals   *6*
   *Various Perspectives*   6
   *Different Styles*   6
Definition Provides Clues   *7*
   *Focus on Purpose*   7
   *Formal Allocation Criteria*   7
Unit Measures   *8*
   *Unit Cost*   8
   *Units-per-Cost*   8
   *Unit Times*   8
Investment Returns   *9*
   *New Benefits Comparison*   9
   *Marginal Productivity*   10
   *Benefit Estimation*   10
Communications   *11*
   *Literary Criterion*   11
   *Audience Requirements*   11
   *Issue Focus*   11
   *Interpretation*   11
   *Integration of Forms*   11

**UNIT 2: Format**   13
The Budgetary Significance of Classification   *13*
   *Play a Legislative Role*   13
   *A Commodity Format*   13

The Exercise    14
- *The Budget Reclassified*    17
- *Performance Format*    17
- *Compare Questions Lists*    21
- *Expenditure Analysis*    21
- *Performance Analysis*    21
- *Classification Schemes*    21
- *The Format Issue*    22
- *Eleven Elements of a Model Budget*    23
- *Write Up Your Specifications List*    23

Elements of a Model Budget    23
- *Investments*    23
- *Financing Plan*    23
- *Estimated Benefits*    27
- *Goal Statement*    27
- *Performance Data*    27
- *Cross-Classification*    29
- *Unit-Cost Calculations*    29
- *Current-Year Experience*    29
- *Benefit Interpretation*    29
- *Investment Return*    29
- *Projections*    29
- *Eclecticism: The Rule*    33
- *A Concluding Note*    33

## UNIT 3: Allocation Criteria: Unit Measures    35

Input-Output Linkages    35
- *Key Tasks*    35
- *Unit Cost*    35
- *Sample Calculation*    36
- *Measures of Performance*    36
- *Comparisons*    37
- *Limitations*    37
- *Fixed and Variable Expenses*    38
- *Subsidiary Unit Costs*    38
- *Unit Times*    38

Exercise: Unit Costs    39

Special Focuses of Unit Measures    49
- *Two Considerations*    49
- *Technology*    49
- *Peak Loads*    50

## UNIT 4: Allocation Criteria: Investment Returns    53

Production Function of Public Budgets    53
- *Formula*    53
- *Diminishing Returns*    53

*Toward a Single End   54*
  *Toward Different Ends   56*
  *Equity Considerations   56*
  *Estimating Benefits   57*
  *Weighting-and-Scoring Models   57*

## UNIT 5: Budget Formulation   61

Format Specifications   61
  *Issue-Paper Structure   61*
  *Instructions   62*
Animal Control in Centerville: An Exercise in Budget Formulation   62
  *The Setting   62*
  *The Warden's Dilemma   67*
  *Your Assignment   68*
Budget Formulation Guidelines   73
  *Diagnostic Focus   73*
Diagnosis: The Preliminary Work   73
  *Loosen Up Your Thinking   73*
  *Conventional Problem Statements May Mislead   73*
  *Action Research   74*
  *The Achilles' Heel of Policy   74*
Concluding the Diagnostic Phase   75
  *Problem Definition and Goal   75*
  *Target Population   75*
  *Performance Criteria   76*
Analytical Phase: The Study of Alternatives   76
  *Impacts and Benefits   77*
  *Multiyear Projections   78*
  *Rejected Alternatives   78*

## UNIT 6: Budget Adoption   79

A Generic Process   79
  *Selective Approach Favored   79*
The Exercise   80
  *Financing Issues   83*
  *Investment Issues   84*
  *Balance Your Budget   84*
  *Make Notes   84*

## Assessment Essay   87

Summing Up   87

*Glossary   91*

# A NOTE TO TEACHERS AND STUDENTS

### TEACHING PRACTICE

Although institutional and political aspects rightly dominate the coursework of public budgeting, most teachers strive to provide students with some exposure to the technical side of the subject.

Based on a sampling of syllabi, budgeting instructors experiment a good deal with the teaching of technique, using a mix of cases, exercises, simulations, and fieldwork. They appear to search for materials and experiences which (1) define the state of the art and (2) illuminate the interplay between politics and technique.

Depending on the instructor's pedagogical disposition, the crowded syllabi of budgeting courses differ markedly in topic sequence, with student exposure to techniques either concentrated at one point or diffused. In addition, teacher perceptions of student interest and learning readiness influence the selection of technical materials and experiences, regulating the coverage and difficulty of offerings.

### WORKBOOK CRITERIA

This brief assessment of teaching practice provides us with certain guidelines for a workbook on the technical side of public budgeting:

- A workbook should be sharply focused. Sharply focused expositions and exercises (1) reduce potential duplication of materials in crowded syllabi and (2) facilitate analysis of the impact of techniques on other values. Thus, only consequential techniques—that is, techniques which would, if practiced proficiently, alter allocation decisions—should be selected for exposition.
- A workbook should be compact. If it is to complement texts and readings dealing with the broader aspects of public bud-

geting, a workbook on budgetary technique must displace as little time and material as possible.
- A workbook should be modular. Each section should be a complete unit dealing with a clearly defined topic. A modular workbook permits instructors to assign these free-standing units in any sequence consistent with their syllabi and the learning readiness of their students.

## FOCUS

Budgetmaking concentrated on four technical concepts of consequence:

- formats
- unit measures
- investment returns
- issue papers

The associated exercises encourage teachers and students to speculate about the policy ramifications of each technique. For example, the workbook provides an exercise in classification which can be used to examine the linkage between formats, allocations, and the influence of interest groups. Indeed, the workbook as a whole should be used to focus student attention on the important issue of technical neutrality, that is, the degree to which budget procedures influence budget decisions.

## COMPACTNESS

Brevity is a virtue of *Budgetmaking*. This compactness reflects the assumption that the typical syllabus allots only about 25 percent of coursework to the technical side of budgeting. The exercises may be conducted by group work in class or individually as written submissions. In particular, the exercises dealing with budget formulation and review can be satisfactorily conducted by small groups using easel charts to register and present their solutions.

## MODULARITY

Although the expositions and exercises of *Budgetmaking* are sequential, its units may be assigned independently and in different order. Of course, a stress on modularity engenders a certain amount of repetition. Where such repetitiveness seemed unduly burdensome, cross-references have been used to reduce redundancy.

The benchmark and assessment essays are exceptions to the modularity rule. To have the desired effect, these two exercises should be executed at the beginning and at the end of the course, respectively. Note that these essays are included to promote student self-clarification. They are not designed for inspection or grading, although instructors should encourage students to discuss their ideas in class, immediately following the composition of each essay.

## ACKNOWLEDGMENTS

In the preparation of *Budgetmaking,* the author drew freely upon his previous work, with the kind permission of the publishers. In this regard, special thanks accrue to the Municipal Finance Officers Association, publishers of *Simplified Governmental Budgeting.* Thanks are also due the following people, who critically read earlier drafts of *Budgetmaking:* S. Kenneth Howard of the U.S. Advisory Commission on Intergovernmental Relations, Douglas Fox of Western Connecticut State University, Michael White of the University of Southern California, Dianne N. Long of California Polytechnic State University–San Luis Obispo, and Gloria Grizzle of Florida State University.

*Edward A. Lehan*

# BUDGETMAKING

## A Workbook of Public Budgeting Theory and Practice

# Benchmark Essay

**CLARIFY YOUR THINKING**

Before beginning your study of this workbook, take a few moments to crystallize your thoughts on the subject of budgeting. To assist you in this effort, draft a short essay in response to the question, What is good budgeting? Page 3 has been set aside for this purpose.

# What Is Good Budgeting?

# UNIT 1
# What Is Good Budgeting?

**NOT AN EASY QUESTION**

Now that you have completed the essay on good budgeting, examine it with critical eyes. Is your definition of good budgeting to the point? Did you clearly establish your standards of judgment?

By all means, share your thoughts about good and bad budgeting with your fellow students and your instructor. You will discover that they hold a surprising variety of viewpoints on the definition of budgeting and the criteria of good practice. Many of these differences will become noteworthy as you progress through this workbook, so jot them down for future reference.

If, after a review of your benchmark essay and the subsequent classroom discussion, you feel that you did not do too well, take heart. Today, even experienced budgetmakers find it hard to agree on a definition of their subject, and harder still to determine the criteria of good practice. Their uncertainty stems from 30 years of experimentation with formats and procedures, which spawned several schools of thought instead of a single concept of best practice. Although this experimentation has been altogether a good thing, a sign of vigor and progress, the resulting semantic and procedural diversity is bothersome not only to experienced practitioners of the craft, but to students as well. No matter how difficult the task, however, budgetmakers must think through the premises of their craft to establish criteria for the evaluation of their work.

## ANOTHER CHANCE

At the end of this workbook, you will find an assessment essay, which once again asks, What is good budgeting? Thus, you will get another chance to deal with this important question. But first, study the material in this workbook; it is designed to help you improve the quality of your initial essay.

A discussion of good budgeting follows. After defining budgeting, it advances three criteria for your consideration.

## LOOKING FOR FUNDAMENTALS

**Various Perspectives**

If we were to ask an economist, a student of politics, an elected chief executive, and a city finance director to define good budgeting, we would discover that budgets—and budgeting—mean different things to different people. The economist would probably dwell on the concept of marginal productivity, and the student of politics on the relationship of budgets to civic morale. The elected chief executive would most likely concentrate on the political ramifications of taxes and appropriations, and the finance director on the virtue of accurate, balanced estimates.

If we took our question to the streets, the average citizen would probably reply that a good budget includes favored programs, but is "too high" as an aggregate of all programs.

These five viewpoints reflect different interests. If we are to establish valid criteria, we must search for fundamentals among these viewpoints.

**Different Styles**

In addition to differences in perspective and interest, we must sort through the semantic and procedural variations associated with the five different types of budgeting:

- line-item budget (LIB)
- performance budget (PerB)
- program budget (ProB)
- planning/programming/budgeting system (PPBS)
- zero-base budget (ZBB)

You must master these terms. Consult the glossary on p. 91 for extended definitions of these five concepts and for other terms which form the budgetmaker's basic vocabulary.

In line-item budgeting, the most traditional type, the actual items of expenditure are frequently summarized by object classifications, such as personal services, supplies, other services and charges, and capital outlays. These summary classifications serve to eliminate the display of commodity lists in published budgets.

A line-item budget tends to concentrate on expenditure analysis, that is, the study of commodities to be bought and their costs. The other four types of budgeting represent alternatives to line-item budgeting.

## DEFINITION PROVIDES CLUES

**Focus on Purpose**

Although the alternatives require different techniques, all four agree on this important point: *Budget procedures and documents should concentrate on what is to be done (i.e., output) or achieved (i.e., outcome), rather than on what is to be bought (i.e., input).*

In addition to stressing purposes, the four alternatives to line-item budgeting tend to concentrate on options, thus directly engaging budgetmakers in the essential task of budgeting: that is, the authoritative rationing of scarce resources. After all, budgeting implies scarcity. (If we have enough to go around, why bother budgeting?) By incorporating techniques promoting the examination of options, the four alternatives foster the development of formal, rather than pragmatic, allocation criteria.

**Formal Allocation Criteria**

Accordingly, we can define *budgeting* as *the purposeful distribution of scarce resources.* This definition suggests three criteria of good budgeting:

- unit measures
- investment returns
- literary quality

Unit measures and investment returns deal directly with the rationing principle of budgeting; literary quality refers to the issues of information and audience.

Because rationing is the essential characteristic of budgeting, the quality of a budget, in whole or in part, depends on (1) the relationship of resources to purposes (the less the better) and (2) the comparative worth of purposes (the more the better).

## UNIT MEASURES

Budgetmakers find that unit measures provide the best means of relating resources to purposes, and input to output.

**Unit Cost**

Unit measures involve the division of input by output, or the reverse. The most popular measure is unit cost:

$$\text{Unit cost} = \frac{\text{Investment}}{\text{Output}}$$

with output expressed in terms of products, work volumes, job or task orders, proportions, indexes, time lags, and so on.

The 1977 budget of the city of Savannah displayed an extensive array of unit costs, including the cost of investigating crimes against persons. Based on an expected work load of 920 crimes, the city allotted $158,397; each investigation was thus estimated to cost $172.17. Check this figure by applying the unit-cost formula to the allotment and workload figures:

$$\$172.17 = \frac{\$158,397}{920}$$

**Units-per-Cost**

The reciprocal of a unit cost is units-per-cost, in which the output is divided by the investment:

$$\text{Units-per-cost} = \frac{\text{Output}}{\text{Investment}}$$

Usually found in cost-effectiveness data arrays, this type of calculation facilitates output comparisons, rather than cost comparisons.

Using the Savannah figures and applying the cost-effectiveness formula, we find that the city was expecting 5.8 investigations per each $1,000 of investment.

**Unit Times**

To concentrate on capital/labor issues or technological possibilities, and to avoid the distorting impact of inflation on unit costs, many budgetmakers use unit times:

$$\text{Unit times} = \frac{\text{Staff hours}}{\text{Output}}$$

Budgets which are formulated and displayed with unit measures help budgetmakers to ration the amount of resources allocated to any given goal. An emphasis on unit measures often promotes experimentation with production techniques and technology. These features thus make unit measures an important criterion of good budgeting.

Although unit measures help us to compare the means of achievement, they shed no light on the comparative worth of any given purpose. To assess the comparative worth of the various purposes supported by a budget, budgetmakers must have a concept of investment returns.

## INVESTMENT RETURNS

The relative worth of any particular purpose (e.g., a goal, program, activity) depends on a comparison of its net return with the returns which could be earned by other purposes competing for the same funds. The rate of an investment return is expressed as net benefits (gross benefits minus the total investment) or as a percentage:

**Net Benefits Comparison**

$$\text{Rate of return} = \frac{\text{Net benefits}}{\text{Investment}}$$

At this point, study Exhibit 1, which shows a model array for investment return comparisons. Budgetmakers faced with competing

EXHIBIT 1. Investment Return Comparisons: A Model Array

| Cost Centers | Gross Benefits | (−) Total Investment | = Net Benefits | Investment Return |
|---|---|---|---|---|
| Code enforcement | + but ? | $139,420 | ? | ? |
| Home care | $249,000 | 70,000 | $179,000 | 256% |
| Animal control | 36,500 | 31,145 | 5,355 | 17% |
| Program *n* | ? | ? | ? | ? |
| Total | ? | ? | ? | ? |

budget proposals are well advised to organize and work with such an array.

By establishing investment-return comparisons, budgetmakers can focus their attention on the input-output relationships of competing programs. For example, if the minimum acceptable rate of return has been established at 20 percent (known as an *admissibility criterion*), the funding of the animal-control program in Exhibit 1 would be questionable, pending a redesign of production techniques to improve its rate of return.

In cases in which benefits are believed to be considerable (e.g., code enforcement) but technically difficult to ascribe, the budgetmaker can use the notation *+ but ?* to indicate that the benefit is positive but unknown. This notation can be supported with a commentary concerning the "unmeasurable" benefits.

By using data arrays similar to that in Exhibit 1, budgetmakers expand their capacity to support an array of programs and/or activities which can produce the highest total return for a given expenditure aggregation.

## Marginal Productivity

When the estimation of benefits is too difficult, budgetmakers should search for quantified output measures, because they can be used in comparisons of marginal productivity—that is, in studies of how increments of investment (in contrast to total investment) affect outputs. In theory, this method is not as efficient as net benefit comparisons; however, it does help to identify investments which increase the rate of output, in contrast to investments which produce declining output rates.

## Benefit Estimation

Every appropriation represents an investment which should produce benefits equal to, or exceeding, its cost. In practice, budgetmakers find benefit estimation the most challenging problem of budgetary practice, because it is beset by many conceptual, as well as practical, difficulties. Diligent budgetmakers work to enlarge the number of programs and activities which can be evaluated by means of investment criteria. This requires the development and maintenance of (1) an appropriate data base emphasizing program impacts and benefits, and (2) a planning and analytical capability.

If budgetmakers establish and maintain benefit estimation models and actively search for evidence, they can satisfactorily identify benefits for a wide range of services.

## COMMUNICATIONS

When adopted, a budget represents a contract between policymakers and administrators. Because budget documents embody certain understandings about future behavior, they should reflect literary, rather than accounting or public relations, standards. Bringing the form and content of budget documents under critical review involves several considerations.

**Literary Criterion**

*First, budget documents should be compact and readable.* Budgetmakers should avoid abstract language and minutiae, and they should test all exhibits and commentary for relevance. In addition, they should provide significant facts rather than generalizations. From a literary point of view, a good budget permits legislators and citizens to grasp its service and goal-attainment implications without having to refer to other sources.

**Audience Requirements**

The rule of relevance is often ignored. Performance data arrays are frequently carried forward from year to year, showing unexplained variations in work loads and goal attainment. Furthermore, these variations often are not related to variations in associated expenditures and revenues. And, in a disturbing number of cases, performance data are aggregated on a calendar-year basis in a budget for a different fiscal period, making it impossible to strike a unit cost to relate expenditures to work loads or performance goals.

*Second, the budgetmaker's skill in topic selection and emphasis determines the literary quality of the budget documents.* One should not slavishly reproduce the chart of accounts in public budget documents nor standardize it from year to year, both of which are widespread vices. Expenditure and revenue arrays should relate to issues, rather than to organizational units or accounting charts. Obviously, if a budget is to relate to issues, its organization must be flexible, particularly in the structure of expenditure and revenue titles. As issues change from year to year, so must the format. It should also be noted that the structure of the titles determines the number of performance exhibits and commentaries, and thus the size and content of the budget document.

**Issue Focus**

*Third, every data array deserves interpretation.* This rule ensures the formal relationship of expenditures and revenues to work loads and

**Interpretation**

goals. Unfortunately, this rule is not firmly established. As a result, budget documents frequently contain page after page of tabular material on expenditures and work loads that does not include explanation or interpretation.

**Integration of Forms**

*Finally, the format and content of a published budget influence the format and content of the supporting records and procedures, as well as the quality of budgetary thought.* By using formats appropriately, document designers can help to diffuse the literary ideals of good budgeting throughout an organization.

Unit 2 elaborates on these important considerations by presenting a model of expenditure interpretation (see Exhibit 5). This model features tightly coordinated displays of expenditures, revenues, related work loads, goal expectations, and ascribed benefits.

# UNIT 2
# Format

## THE BUDGETARY SIGNIFICANCE OF CLASSIFICATION

The human mind never ceases to classify the manifold facts of life. This ability to classify provides the foundation of human knowledge, a basis for individual understanding, and a vehicle for social communication.

In the preface to his classic, *Government Budgeting* (1956), Jesse Burkhead pointed out the budgetary significance of classification schemes when he stated "the way in which revenue and expenditure are grouped for decision-making is the most important aspect of budgeting."

An exercise in classification starts on p. 14. In this exercise, imagine that you are a legislator in a jurisdiction of 70,000 people at budget adoption time. The chief executive has submitted a proposed annual budget, and it is now under consideration by the legislature. You must examine the code enforcement budget in preparation for a workshop session with responsible personnel.

**Play a Legislative Role**

Study the code enforcement budget presented in Exhibit 2. Note that it is classified by things to be bought. The categories of *personal*

**A Commodity Format**

**EXHIBIT 2.** A Line-Item Budget (Summarized by Object Classes)

| *Current-Year Estimate* | *Code Enforcement* | *Budget* | *% Change* |
|---|---|---|---|
| $ 98,430 | Personal services | $120,475 | +22.4 |
| 2,245 | Supplies | 2,750 | +22.5 |
| 17,575 | Other services and charges | 15,725 | −10.5 |
|  | Capital outlay | 470 |  |
| $118,250 |  | $139,420 | +17.9 |

*services, supplies, other services and charges,* and *capital outlays* are known as *object classes*. Each object class acts as a summary description of appropriate items of expenditure. The *personal services* classification embraces the costs of regular payrolls, overtime payments, employee benefits, and so on. Stationery, fuel, and small tools, for example, fall under the concept of *supplies*. *Other services and charges* include printing, postage, and professional contracts. *Capital outlay* sums up the costs of equipment, machinery, and other additions to fixed assets.

Because the code enforcement appropriation of $139,420, is divided into object classes, the expenditure array in Exhibit 2 is an example of a line-item budget. Note that this budget does not include narrative displays, performance data, or any other material which could help justify and interpret the expenditures. Typically, line-item budgets do not provide such documentation.

## THE EXERCISE

Keeping in mind that you are a legislator preparing for a budget workshop with your colleagues and the responsible administrators, study the expenditure array again. As questions come to mind, jot them down in the space provided on p. 15.

PERSONAL SERVICES, $120,475

SUPPLIES, $2,750

OTHER SERVICES AND CHARGES, $15,725

CAPITAL OUTLAY, $470

Next, study the code enforcement budget presented in Exhibit 3. It is the same budget as that shown in Exhibit 2, but it is classified differently. The same expenditures are planned, but they are summarized by concepts which indicate things to be done or sought, instead of things to be bought.

**The Budget Reclassified**

EXHIBIT 3. A Performance Budget (Summarized by Activities)

| Current-Year Estimate | Code Enforcement | Budget | % Change |
|---|---|---|---|
| $ 28,645 | Leadership | $ 31,050 | + 8.4 |
| 23,010 | Plan Examination | 24,660 | + 7.2 |
| 65,595 | Inspection | 80,680 | +23.0 |
|  | Innovation | 1,700 |  |
| 1,000 | Education | 1,330 | +33.0 |
| $118,250 |  | $139,420 | +17.9 |

The categories of leadership, plan examination, inspection, innovation, and education are known as *activity classes, cost centers,* or both. Now, turn your attention to Exhibit 4, which presents workload data for the inspection cost center. The combination of activity classes and associated workload data makes this budget a performance budget.

**Performance Format**

Again, pretend you are a legislator preparing for a budget workshop. Jot down your questions about this reclassified budget in the space provided on p. 19.

EXHIBIT 4. A Performance Data Array

| Current-Year Estimate | Code Enforcement | Budget | % Change |
|---|---|---|---|
| $65,595 | Inspection investment | $80,680 | +23.0 |
| 9,430 | Inspections | 11,025 | +16.9 |
| 1,735 | Permits | 1,865 | + 7.5 |
| 6,760 | Hours | 8,320 | +23.1 |
| $6.96 | Investment/inspections | $7.32 | + 5.2 |
| 5.44 | Inspections/permits | 5.91 | + 8.6 |
| 1.40 | Inspections/hours | 1.33 | – 5.0 |

LEADERSHIP, $31,050

PLAN EXAMINATION, $24,660

INSPECTION, $80,680

INNOVATION, $1,700

EDUCATION, $1,330

Now, compare your two question lists from pp. 15 and 19. They should differ significantly. This is an example of the power of a format to influence thinking—and possibly budget allocations.

**Compare Question Lists**

Commodity-oriented budgets normally encourage the traditional form of expenditure analysis—that is, an inquiry into the increases and decreases of particular objects or object classes. Recall that in Exhibit 2, the object classification, personal services, increased by $22,045, or 22.4%. By means of traditional expenditure analysis, this difference would be explained in the following way:

**Expenditure Analysis**

| | | |
|---:|---|---|
| $ 98,430 | | *Current-Year Revised Estimate* |
| 4,805+ | | Effect of pay-plan amendment |
| 1,040+ | | Merit increment |
| 230+ | | Additional week of vacation coverage |
| 40+ | | Additional cost of 4 weeks of vacation coverage due to pay-plan amendment increasing temporary hourly pay rate from $5.75 to $6.00 |
| 15,600+ | | One additional inspector position to cope with work load |
| 330+ | | Overtime payments for producing revised code |
| $120,475 | | *Proposed Budget* |

Critics of the commodity-oriented format point out that it invites thought and discussion about things to be bought, rather than stimulating concern with policy and procedure. Furthermore, a commodity display often tempts the reviewing officials to alter the expenditure pattern in ways unrelated to policy issues, service levels, or both. Too often, such changes—usually reductions—are not even accompanied by explanations or expressions of intent.

In contrast, the data arrays of the reclassified code enforcement budget invite those reviewing it to consider the relationship of expenditures to work loads and public goals. This type of budget draws attention to such issues as code updating; the tempo, quality, and techniques of inspection; and the effort put into the education of inspection personnel, the regulated interests, and the public.

**Performance Analysis**

In order to understand and assess the terms used to identify expenditures and revenues, you will find it helpful to survey a sample of budget documents drawn from various state and local jurisdic-

**Classification Schemes**

tions. In doing so, you will find that budgetmakers use a substantial number of concepts. Furthermore, you will discover that these conceptions can be assigned to general categories, or classification "families." The following table presents 29 concepts which were found in various budget documents.

| Organization | Accounting | Configuration | Performance | Policy |
|---|---|---|---|---|
| Office, agency, department, division, bureau section, and unit | Fund, account, cost center, object, and item | Class, category, component, element, and the use of the prefix *sub-*, as in *subcomponent* | Function, activity, task, job, responsibility center, time, and space (area) | Goal, objective, service, program, and project |

A survey of classification schemes will usually show that budgetmakers mix their identifiers, drawing terms from more than one classification family. For example, organizational terms are often associated with accounting and performance concepts, as shown in the following exhibit drawn from the 1983-84 budget of the city of Chelsea, Massachusetts.

| Classification Concept | Classification Family | Example |
|---|---|---|
| Fund | Accounting | General |
| Function | Performance | Public safety |
| Department | Organization | Police |
| Activity | Performance | Patrols |
| Object | Accounting | Compensation |

With the widespread availability of computer technology, budgetmakers are expanding the number of classifications which can be assigned to any given expenditure or revenue. This capability makes it possible to prepare and execute budgets with multiple formats.

## The Format Issue

Narrative budgets are now fairly common. By and large, however, the typical public budget document is an accounting statement, crammed with numbers intelligible only to those who prepared them. In terms of the literary criterion advanced in Unit 1, format development is a relatively uncharted frontier.

In Unit 1, we pointed out that the communications quality of a budget document depends on topic selection and emphasis. Moreover, we noted that topics and the supporting narratives and data arrays should reflect the underlying analytical work.

Unfortunately, classification schemes are often prescribed by law or set by a central authority. In addition, to ensure comparability, classification schemes may be standardized and extended over many fiscal years. Yet, each expenditure pattern is unique, with ever-changing presentation requirements. As a result, rigid, standardized classification schemes work strongly against effective budgeting. Although comparability is valuable, it is much more important to concentrate budgetmaking attention on problems and opportunities. In any given year, this may mean an increase or decrease in expenditure classifications, depending on the number of titles needed to illuminate the issues.

Exhibit 5 presents an annotated model format, the topic of which is home care, a local-government health service. As you will see, this model has 11 elements, or specifications. These reflect the criteria of good budgeting established in Unit 1. **Eleven Elements of a Model Budget**

Before you begin to study the model budget, take a moment to consolidate your thoughts about the specifications of a public budget document. Use the space provided on p. 25 to jot down specifications which seem important to you. **Write Up Your Specifications List**

Now, study the model budget displayed in Exhibit 5 on pp. 27 and 28, comparing its elements with your specifications.

## ELEMENTS OF A MODEL BUDGET

The data array presenting the allocation is, of course, the most fundamental part of any budget presentation. This array, marked 1 in the model in Exhibit 5, shows the amount(s) to be invested, or spent, and the purpose. Although not shown in the model, the sum to be invested is often divided into subsidiary "cost centers," each of which is, in itself, a summary of subsidiary aggregations. **Investments**

The financing plan (2) calls attention to the sources of financial support. Obviously, the total of this data array must equal the total of the proposed investments. In cases in which revenue exceeds the budget, the excess should be shown negatively, and the excess should be assigned to another budget. **Financing Plan**

MY SPECIFICATIONS FOR A MODEL BUDGET ARE:

1.

2.

3.

4.

5.

6.

7.

8.

9.

10.

11.

**EXHIBIT 5. A Model Budget**

**BUDGET**

**① INVESTMENTS**

| | |
|---|---|
| Home care | $70,000 |

**② FINANCING PLAN**

| | |
|---|---|
| Private grant | $ 7,000 |
| Service charges | 61,600 |
| Property taxes | 1,400 |
| | $70,000 |

**③ ESTIMATED BENEFITS**

| | |
|---|---|
| Cost avoidance | $224,000 |
| Patient productivity | 30,000 |
| Patient comfort | + but ? |
| | $254,000 |

④ *PLANS FOR BUDGET YEAR.* Started last year as an efficient, less costly alternative to institutionalized care for stroke and fracture victims, a home care team, on contract from the ABC Rehabilitation Center, expects to deliver coordinated therapeutic services to an estimated 220 persons, an increase of 20:

**⑤**

| This Year | Performance Indicator | Budget |
|---|---|---|
| 200 | Cases | 220 |

As an estimated 300 residents could benefit from home care, the service will reach 73 percent of its target.

Stroke and fracture victims predominate among referrals from physicians and area hospitals. With stroke and fracture victims, physical and speech therapists aim at self-care and, beyond that, economic productivity. With patients deemed chronically ill and/or disabled, the home care team provides services to make them comfortable. In the following cross-classification, the home care budget is allocated to impact categories that reflect these objectives:

*IMPACTS*

| | *Reducing Personal Dependency* | *Reducing Economic Dependency* | *General Welfare* | *Total* |
|---|---|---|---|---|
| ⑥ Investments | $20,950 | $28,800 | $20,250 | $70,000 |
| Cases | 70 | 60 | 90 | 220 |
| ⑦ Unit cost | $ 299 | $ 480 | $ 225 | $ 318 |

---

Estimated benefits (3) provides information on the benefits to be produced by the proposed resource allocation. Ascribed benefits should equal or exceed the investment. In cases in which benefits cannot be monetized, the budgetmaker can indicate the tendency of the benefit, positive or negative, and the fact that its value is unknown, by using the following shorthand: *+ but ?* or *– but ?*

**Estimated Benefits**

The first paragraphs of a budget commentary (4) should define the problem(s) or issue(s) addressed by the budget, and set forth performance targets. The performance data array (5) should be placed within the context of the problem definition and goal statement, and reference to it should be encouraged.

**Goal Statement**

**Performance Data**

# EXHIBIT 5 (cont.)

**⑧** In the current year, at 200 cases, the service is reaching 67 percent of its expected potential. Current-year investments are estimated at $65,000, yielding a unit cost of $325. Reflecting scale economies, next year's case load of 220 will reduce unit costs by 2 percent.

**⑨ ESTIMATED BENEFITS.** Total benefits ascribed to the investment in home care, are estimated to equal, or exceed, $254,000, indicating a net benefit of $184,000.

In 70 cases, costing $20,950, the therapeutic effort is aimed at improving the patient's capability for self-care, eliminating an estimated 600 days of institutionalized care @ $100, or $60,000, and 600 days of home nursing care @ $40, or $24,000. Benefits exceed cost by $63,050.

In 60 cases, costing $28,800, the patient has the potential to work again. Home care will eliminate 500 days of institutional care @ $100, or $50,000, and, in addition, may claim a certain amount of economic impact by promoting a more rapid rate of recovery. Ten working days per patient @ $50 are regarded as a fair estimate of the economic gain due home care.

Total estimated benefits of $80,000, exceed investment by $51,200.

In 90 cases, costing $20,250, the aim is to make the patient as comfortable as possible. No significant gains in either self-care or economic productivity are expected. In these cases, home care eliminates an estimated 900 days of hospital or convalescent care @ $100, or $90,000, this benefit exceeding costs by $69,750.

**⑪ MULTIYEAR PERSPECTIVE.** Over the next five years, the home care service is expected to reach its target of 300 cases per year. At that scale of operations, unit costs (assuming no inflation) should drop to an estimated $300, yielding an annual investment level of $90,000, offset by service charges of $84,000.

At that scale of operations, the taxpayer subsidy drops to zero, and the grant from the XYZ Foundation decreases to $6,000.

As the break-even point for full self-financing is estimated to be 500 cases, elimination of foundation support cannot occur unless service charges are increased beyond the current $280 case average.

**⑩ RETURN ON INVESTMENT**

| | |
|---|---:|
| Unneeded institutional care | $200,000 |
| Unneeded nursing care | 24,000 |
| Patient productivity | 30,000 |
| Patient comfort | + but ? |
| Gross benefit | 254,000 |
| Less investment | 70,000 |
| Net benefit | $184,000 |
| Return on investment | 263% |

Budgetmakers use cross-classifications (6) to explore the dimensions of an investment proposal, highlighting and emphasizing its linkages and multiple values. The distribution of proposed investments to impact categories, as shown in the model, is helpful in isolating portions of a proposed allocation for special studies of unit costs (7) and marginal productivity.

**Cross-Classification**

**Unit-Cost Calculations**

Although the cost-center array in Exhibit 5 did not display historical comparisons, it is sometimes useful to refer to current- and prior-year experience, as shown in the model (8).

**Current-Year Experience**

A commentary on estimated benefits (9), referencing the data array, should provide insight into key assumptions and calculations, setting the stage for the discussion of investment returns (10).

**Benefit Interpretation**

**Investment Return**

A multiyear forecast—in this case, 5 years—is the final element of the model budget. Multiyear projections (11) help budget reviewers and policymakers to get an idea of the future implications of adopting the proposed budget.

**Projections**

At this point, you should record your reactions to the model budget. Use the space provided below to settle the points of difference between your specifications and the elements of the model budget. For example, in contrast to the model, your specifications might call for expenditure detail, such as salaries and travel expense. Indicate whether you still wish to incorporate that type of information.

**Eclecticism: The Rule**

As pointed out in Unit 1, budgetmakers have developed five styles of budgeting: line-item budgeting, performance budgeting, program budgeting, planning/programming/budgeting system, and zero-base budgeting. Each is distinguished by its format, supporting procedures, and analytical techniques. In Unit 1, you were encouraged to consult the glossary to learn more about these styles. Now, as we conclude our discussion of formats, look up these terms again. Then, examine the model budget with these five styles in mind. Which three concepts does the model budget utilize?

**A Concluding Note**

Budgetmakers do not regard formats with neutrality. Rather, they believe that in pure form, each format produces (or reflects) a unique ethos, or policy bearing. It is believed that the practice of line-item budgeting flourishes in environments dominated by control and economy values. Performance budgeting and zero-base budgeting, on the other hand, are thought to express official interest in management and efficiency values. Finally, officials interested in planning and goal achievement seem to favor program budgeting and planning/programming/budgeting system procedures.

*Remember,* formats are important! People tend to think about that which is put before them.

# UNIT 3
# Allocation Criteria: Unit Measures

**INPUT-OUTPUT LINKAGES**

In Unit 1, you learned that public budgeting is more than the pricing of commodities. It is also a thought process about rationing which seeks (1) to relate public resources to public purposes and (2) to assess whether these purposes are worthy of public support. Unit 2 explored the way budgetmakers use formats to pursue these two key tasks. In this unit, you will get a chance to work with unit measures.

    Although unit measures are of little use to budgetmakers seeking to determine the relative worth of public purposes, they are quite valuable in linking inputs to outputs for any given purpose. Because they require the assembly of output data, these simple calculations encourage the development of measures of performance (MOP). In addition, unit measures promote efficient production by centering attention on peak loads and the application of labor-saving, energy-using technology.

**Key Tasks**

Unit measures are produced by dividing outputs and inputs by each other. These simple calculations are useful because they automatically

**Unit Cost**

relate the resources invested in a public purpose to the output. The most popular unit measure is unit cost:

$$\text{Unit cost} = \frac{\text{Investment}}{\text{Output}}$$

where output is expressed in terms of products, work volumes, job or task orders, proportions, time lags, and so on.

**Sample Calculation**

For an example, let's draw on data provided in the animal-control exercise in Unit 5. In the current year, the government of Centerville expects to invest an estimated $19,240 in the impoundment of 730 stray animals. The unit cost of impoundment is calculated as follows:

$$\frac{\$19,240}{730} = \$26.36$$

Although the calculation itself is easy, budgetmakers usually encounter problems in the pursuit of valid performance measures and accurate costs. As a rule, budgetmakers find it easier to assemble costs than output data, principally because financial transactions are subject to stringent, centralized controls, whereas performance information reposes in weakly regulated departmental files, if at all.

**Measures of Performance**

To apply a scheme of unit measures, the budgetmaker must identify a single output indicator for each cost center, or set up a cost center for each output indicator. Each indicator must be measurable and subject to audit-type verification. If possible, the scheme of output indicators should be formally described, and the subsequent tabulations entered into the accounting record with the same care as expenditure data.

The application of the single-indicator-per-cost-center rule determines the scheme of cost centers. In cases where multiple performance measures are to be related to a given investment level, this rule requires the construction of a weighted index that combines various measures into one abstract indicator.

Exhibit 6 presents a sample weighted index of selected recreation activities. The assigned weights of 1/100, 9/100, and 90/100 reveal the relative value placed on the activities of swimming, organized sports, and skill development by the municipal authorities. The graduation of one person from a skill course is deemed 90 times

**EXHIBIT 6. A Sample Performance Index**

| Activity | Measure | Output | Performance Data |
|---|---|---|---|
| Swimming | Participant hours | 15,000 × 0.01 = | 150 |
| Organized sports | Participant hours | 30,000 × 0.09 = | 2,700 |
| Skill development | Graduates | 500 × 0.90 = | 450 |
| | | | 3,300 |

more valuable than an hour of swimming, and 10 times more valuable than an hour of participation in organized sports.

The fact that the weighting requirements of indexing establish budget priorities is considered a desirable result of the indexing procedure. It is likely that weighted performance data will have an impact on managerial motivation, encouraging lines of action which skew the mix of activities to produce higher performance units.

Unit measures can be associated with index numbers. In this case, assuming a recreation investment of $50,000, the program mix reflected in Exhibit 6 results in an output-cost ratio of 66 units per $1,000 and/or a unit cost of $15.15. By maintaining a time series of this index and its subsidiary unit measures, budgetmakers can strive for a mix of highest priority activities at lowest unit cost.

**Comparisons**

Unit measures have no meaning by themselves. They must be compared to other unit measures which are based on similar inputs, outputs, or both. A time series of unit costs, which is frequently featured in performance budgets, is the most popular method of comparison. Comparison of unit costs to "standard" costs is also popular, with the expected cost set up at budget time. In addition, if suppliers and price data are available, unit costs can be profitably compared to the marketplace. Finally, in a given situation, different production techniques can be tested by means of unit-cost comparisons.

**Limitations**

The unit-measures approach has certain limitations. For instance, unit-measure comparisons only apply to "positive" outputs. However, in government, funds are often invested to abate, or eliminate, a public evil or undesired condition, such as crime, fire, disease, and accident. In such a case, the investment is supposed to suppress the thing being counted. If it does, unit costs tend to rise, and conversely, output-cost ratios decline. In lieu of unit measures, in abatement situations, budgetmakers attempt to assess the relative social and economic benefits which accrue to such investments. Unit 4 will present a discussion of allocation criteria based on the concept of investment return.

**Fixed and Variable Expenses**

Unit-cost variations focus attention on the difference between *fixed* and *variable* expenses. Variable expenses usually rise if output rises, and fall if output falls. Fixed costs, also known as *overhead* or *indirect costs,* do not fluctuate with output, at least not over the short run. Of course, over the long run, significant changes in work load may require adjustments in space, equipment, and so on, thus affecting the assignment of fixed costs. Consider the managerial implications: if a scheme of unit measures can be established for variable expenses, program managers can be held strictly accountable for the relationship of variable costs to output. If work loads go down, so should unit costs, and vice versa.

**Subsidiary Unit Costs**

The unit cost of any operation or procedure can often be factored into a set of subsidiary unit costs. In the animal-control example in Unit 5, the unit cost of impoundment, $26.36, is a compound of unit costs for search-and-capture, travel to and from the pound, room and board for the animals, and animal disposal. Each activity might warrant the establishment of a cost center to track expenses and seek economies. Even so, budgetmakers should avoid establishing cost centers, and their associated unit costs, at high levels of aggregation. An extensive scheme of unit costs produces opportunities for minor technical changes which can add up to impressive productivity improvements.

**Unit Times**

In times of currency inflation, unit costs rise with no change in the technique or volume of production. As a result, the value of time-series comparisons is eroded. The budgetmaker could apply price deflators to eliminate the effects of inflation, but it would be at considerable cost and confusion. On the other hand, the budgetmaker could establish a scheme of unit times, relating staff hours to output instead of costs. This would not only sidestep the inflation problem, it would also set up fundamental data bases which encourage the study of productivity in labor-intensive public programs.

We now turn to an exercise in the use of unit costs.

## EXERCISE: UNIT COSTS

Exhibit 7 presents selected cost and performance data for an alcoholic treatment service, including:

- a scheme of treatment concepts, organized as cost centers
- the number of clients to be served
- the hours of professional assistance to be devoted to each treatment concept
- a recommended budget of $100,000, divided into fixed and variable costs

Note that the variable costs have been assigned to cost centers according to the percentage distribution of professional hours. However, the fixed costs—which in this case include payments for administrative and clerical support, supplies, and rent—have not been assigned. The allocation of fixed costs and the selection of a measure of performance (MOP) are left up to you. Once you have established a theory for the allocation of fixed costs, you will be able to derive a set of unit costs for the array of treatment concepts.

As noted, the staff-hour distribution was used as the criterion for the assignment of variable costs. Of course, this criterion may also be used to assign fixed costs. However, you may wish to use the percentage distribution of clients instead, because each client benefits equally from the provision of the alcoholic treatment services.

**EXHIBIT 7. Treatment of Alcoholics: Selected Data**

| Cost Centers | Clients | % | Hours | % | Fixed Costs | Variable Costs |
|---|---|---|---|---|---|---|
| Crisis intervention | 100 | 25% | 600 | 10% | $_____ | $ 6,000 |
| Mutual help groups | 120 | 30% | 1,500 | 25% | _____ | 15,000 |
| Family therapy | 80 | 20% | 2,100 | 35% | _____ | 21,000 |
| Individual counseling | 100 | 25% | 1,800 | 30% | _____ | 18,000 |
| | 400 | | 6,000 | | $40,000 | $60,000 |

After you have settled on a criterion for the assignment of fixed costs to the treatment cost centers, use the space below to describe and justify it.

Now, study Exhibit 8. It provides a worksheet for the calculation of the unit costs of each mode of treatment. Distributing the fixed costs is your first task. If you selected staff hours as your criterion, multiply the percentage of total staff hours devoted to each mode of treatment by the total amount of fixed costs (i.e., by $40,000), and distribute the results by entering them in the appropriate spaces in the fixed-costs column in Exhibit 8. For example, if you selected staff-hours as your criterion, the percentage of fixed costs applied to crisis intervention is 10 percent, resulting in an assignment of $4,000 (10% × $40,000).

Next, add the fixed and variable costs together, and enter these sums in the appropriate spaces in the investment column of Exhibit 8. These sums, which represent the investments in each mode of treatment, should total $100,000.

Assuming that measures of performance are available, you are now ready to calculate unit costs. In this case, the number of clients is an obvious choice as a measure of performance, and by now you should have entered the appropriate figures drawn from Exhibit 7 on the worksheet in Exhibit 8. Do the calculations; then compare the per-client costs of each treatment mode. In pondering this array of unit costs, one might inquire about the efficiency of the different treatment modalities. Furthermore, one might ask about the appropriateness of using the number of clients as the measure of performance. Certainly, if it were available, the number "cured" of alcoholism would provide an even better measure of performance, because its use encourages the budgetmaker to assess the effectiveness of each treatment modality. We will encounter this aspect of the alcoholic treatment problem again in Unit 4.

**EXHIBIT 8. Unit Measures Worksheet**

| Cost Centers | Fixed Costs + | Variable Costs = | Investment ÷ | MOP = | Unit Costs |
|---|---|---|---|---|---|
| Crisis intervention | $_____ | $ 6,000 | $_____ | 100 | $_____ |
| Mutual help groups | _____ | 15,000 | _____ | 120 | _____ |
| Family therapy | _____ | 21,000 | _____ | 80 | _____ |
| Individual counseling | _____ | 18,000 | _____ | 100 | _____ |
| | $40,000 | $60,000 | $100,000 | 400 | |

## SPECIAL FOCUSES OF UNIT MEASURES

As we have seen, budgetmakers use formal relationships, such as unit measures, in order to focus attention on production techniques. In considering such techniques, budgetmakers should maintain a steady interest in the following elements:

- *Technological support,* with attention directed to capital-labor ratios, depreciation, and obsolescence.
- *Workload variations,* with attention directed to peak loads and their influence on staffing patterns.

**Two Considerations**

In general, governments are labor-intensive organizations, slow to take up new technology and slower still to slough off the obsolescent. Despite the centrality of technological factors in labor productivity, the typical government is undercapitalized. Like maintenance expenses, allotments for technology can be put off until next year, and usually are. Although the relationship of capital to labor is a significant focus of thought and action in profit-seeking enterprises, it is rarely used as a formal criterion of allocation in governments. Indeed, the prevailing theory of governmental accounting deemphasizes the concept of depreciation, thus making it difficult to (1) derive accurate unit measures and (2) assess capital-labor ratios.

**Technology**

At this point, review Exhibit 2 on p. 14. The code enforcement budget illustrates the depreciation problem. First, the capital outlay of $470 (providing for a typewriter) will not be amortized over the machine's useful life, but will be charged as a lump sum to the code enforcement budget in the year of purchase. In addition, this budget does not reflect the amortized value of equipment purchased for the code enforcement service in prior years, including motor vehicles, office equipment, and tools. The amortized value of prior-year investments is estimated at $6,970. Furthermore, costs for office space and other overhead charges are not represented in the code enforcement budget of Exhibit 2.

Obviously, the failure to include these charges in the operating budget for code enforcement results in understated unit costs and makes it difficult to assess the impact of technology on labor productivity. On the other hand, when budgets include amortized capital charges, any changes in the assets assigned to any given service alter unit measures of that service.

If the code enforcement budget included capital charges and space costs, those responsible would be encouraged to test the unit-cost impact of changed office layouts, new office technology, and different vehicle-replacement schedules.

As a rule, a jurisdiction's annual investment in technology should equal or exceed the rate at which its assets are depreciating. Budgetmakers therefore have a responsibility to ensure that technological alternatives are prominently considered in budget deliberations.

One way to stimulate interest in the investment issue is to conduct an annual evaluation of the technological basis of production. Such an evaluation should include physical inspection, service-record reviews, and an assessment of contributions to production and goal attainment. When combined with data on technological alternatives, such an audit often leads to a purge of obsolete equipment in favor of state-of-the-art technology.

## Peak Loads

In general, governments are plagued with fluctuating work loads. If, as mentioned in Unit 1, a formal relationship of expenditures to work loads is a criterion of good budgeting, then budgetmakers must pay attention to these variations. For example, in the cities of the snow belt, snow-removal work loads vary unpredictably, as do many service demands which are keyed to seasonal or natural events. Police and fire work loads constantly shift by time and place. Administrative units, such as finance, experience cyclical volumes in assessment, tax collection, and accounting.

At this point, refer to Exhibit 4 on p. 17. It provides a good illustration of the analytical utility of unit measures. Note the fluctuations in the performance ratios. Unit cost is rising, as is performance quality, which is measured by the number of inspections per hour. On the other hand, performance efficiency, measured by the number of inspections per permit, is declining. What is the budgetmaker to make of these incongruities?

If the current inspection-permit ratio of 5.44 is adopted as an acceptable standard, the increase in staff hours will exceed that required by the anticipated increase in permits. However, if no staff hours are added in the budget, the inspection ratio will decline, which is perhaps undesirable. Faced with this issue, a budgetmaker should search for a modulated response. For example, could the increase in work load be met by changes in production techniques—for example, more efficient job routing or reduced paperwork—thus making more inspection time available? The input mix could also be changed by adding temporary help, overtime payments, or both, in lieu of adding a permanent position.

Bringing input and output into an efficient balance is never easy, as the code enforcement example illustrates. In urban areas, fire-suppression services offer an extreme example of rigidly organized resources deployed to cope with unpredictable peak demands. Police deployments and service demands are usually more closely correlated, but, even there, work loads vary sharply by time and place in the face of stable deployment patterns. In contrast, public-works units have somewhat more latitude in using contractors and temporary workers to meet seasonal and emergency demands with a modulated response.

In confronting this challenging problem, budgetmakers must explore the issues of production, using unit measures to encourage the deployment of an appropriate mix of staff, technology, overtime hours, temporary help, and contractual assistance.

# UNIT 4
# Allocation Criteria: Investment Returns

## PRODUCTION FUNCTION OF PUBLIC BUDGETS

As you discovered in your consideration of code enforcement and alcoholic-treatment budgets in Unit 3, the study of unit measures helps a budgetmaker to understand and describe the production functions of public budgets. In mathematical shorthand, the production function of a public budget may be described as follows:

$$y = f(x)$$

where $x$ equals the budget allotment, $y$ equals the public benefit (monetized, if possible; if not, specified in numerical or physical terms), and $f$ denotes the production technique, such as police patrols, inspection, and classroom instruction.

**Formula**

We know that $y$ (the output) generally depends on $x$ (the input) and that the output should increase or decrease as the input increases or decreases. We also know, however, that every investment is subject to the law of diminishing returns, which declares that, after a certain point, more input produces relatively less output. Accordingly, different levels of appropriation for a given program produce different

**Diminishing Returns**

**EXHIBIT 9. The General Curve of Marginal Productivity**

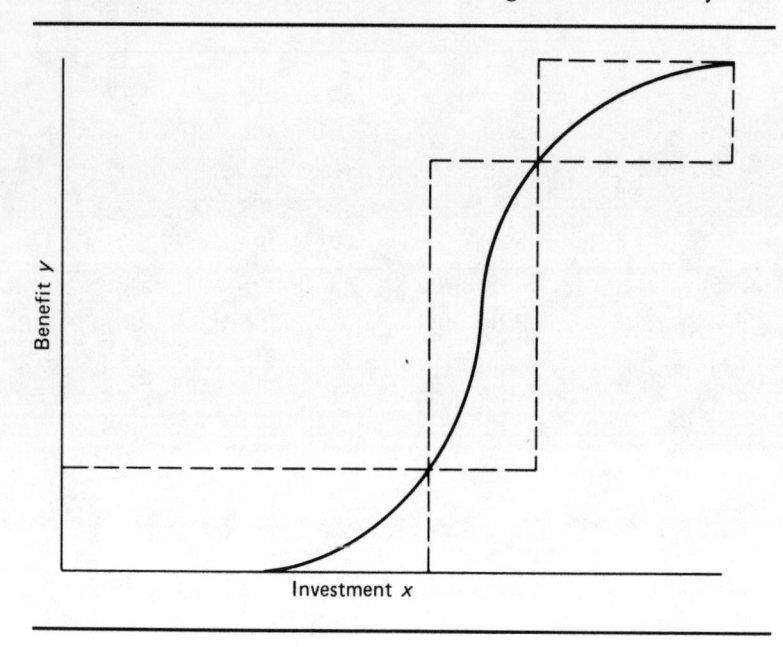

*[Graph showing a lazy S curve with Benefit y on the vertical axis and Investment x on the horizontal axis]*

amounts of benefit. The varying utilities of program investments are graphically described by a "lazy S curve" relating investments to benefits. An abstract example of this lazy S curve is shown in Exhibit 9. By inspecting this curve, we can see that outputs, or benefits, are low at the beginning of an investment aggregation, but rise sharply as the level of investment rises; they begin to level off at the higher end of the investment aggregation, as less and less benefit accrues to the effort. This situation is analogous to the "saturated market" of private enterprise.

Budgetmakers find the concept of the lazy S curve helpful in two ways: First, a budgetmaker thinking in terms of the curve is encouraged to describe and evaluate the relationship between the inputs and outputs of different investments aimed at a *single end*. The alcoholic-treatment service data shown in Exhibit 7 is a good example of such investments. One could place each treatment cost center displayed in the data array of the exhibit on a continuous curve of investment aggregation, with each cost center treated as a marginal investment and matched with the estimated number of clients to be "cured" by that form of treatment.

Exhibit 10 shows the alcoholic-treatment data organized as an input-output schedule, and Exhibit 11 shows the resulting marginal utility curve. Note that, for the purposes of these exhibits, the

**Toward a Single End**

EXHIBIT 10. A Marginal Productivity Schedule: Alcoholic Treatment

|  | Investment | Cumulative Investment | Estimated Cures | Cumulative Cures |
|---|---|---|---|---|
| Crisis intervention | $16,000 | $ 16,000 | 0 | 0 |
| Mutual help groups | 27,000 | 43,000 | 50 | 50 |
| Family therapy | 29,000 | 72,000 | 25 | 75 |
| Individual counseling | 28,000 | 100,000 | 15 | 90 |

$40,000 in fixed costs summarized in Exhibit 7 has been assigned to treatment cost centers according to the number of clients. In addition, note that the number of clients "cured" is used as a surrogate for monetized benefits, which are assumed to be approximately equal for all clients, thus making the use of the surrogate appropriate. Monetized benefits would include allowances for reducing (1) production losses, (2) medical costs, and (3) the suffering of addicts and affected relatives.

An inspection of Exhibits 10 and 11 shows that investments in family therapy and individual counseling yield relatively lower returns than do investments in the mutual-help form of treatment. This suggests that, if less than $100,000 is to be invested in the treatment of

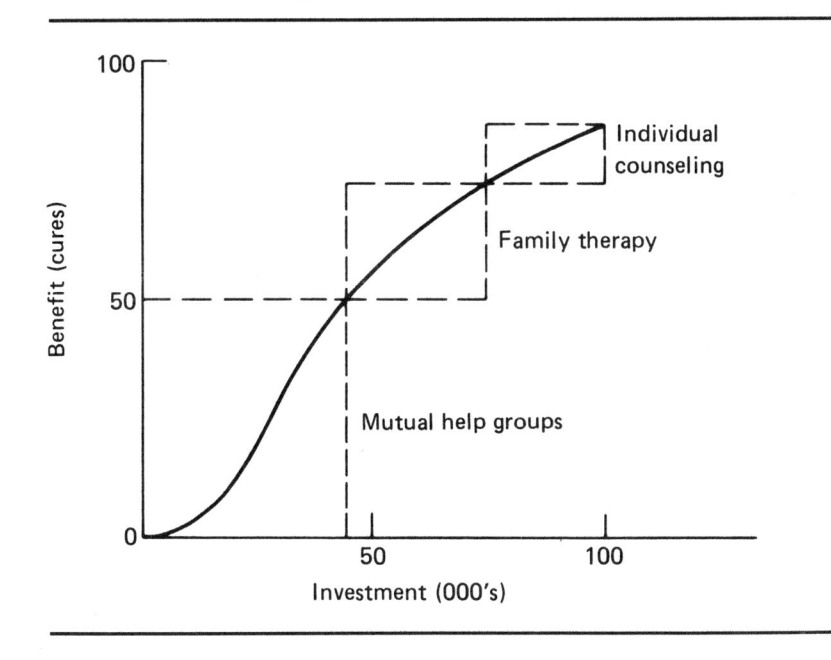

EXHIBIT 11. A Marginal Productivity Curve: Alcoholic Treatment

alcoholics, it should be allocated to the most cost-effective treatment technique(s).

## Toward Different Ends

The concept of the lazy S curve is also helpful to a budgetmaker thinking in terms of the curve of marginal utility because he or she is encouraged to compare the input-output relationships of investments aimed at *different ends,* such as the "cure" of alcoholics versus the language competency of elementary-school children.

In order to compare the relative returns on investments in dissimilar ends, the budgetmaker must establish a common denominator of monetized benefits. If the benefits of investments in dissimilar ends can be estimated and monetized, the budgetmaker can compare net returns in the manner suggested by Exhibit 1 (see p. 9).

In general, the budgetmaker uses the concept of the lazy S curve to locate and recommend investment proposals which produce increasing returns (that is, which are located below the turning point, or margin, of the curve), and to reject those which are associated with diminishing returns (that is, which are located above the margin).

Suppose a budgetmaker cannot monetize and compare net benefits of dissimilar programs (the preferred approach), yet can determine the marginal utility of investments by using output measurements peculiar to each program. The budgetmaker is thus in a position to recommend shifting scarce resources from investments with diminishing utility to those with increasing utility.

Imagine, for example, that a proposed investment in an elementary-school reading program is associated with rising marginal efficiency, as measured by test scores. Putting more resources into this effort would be clearly justified. It would also be appropriate to suggest that funds for the reading program be shifted from the alcoholic-treatment service because more than half of the latter's investment aggregation is associated with diminishing utility, as measured by clients "cured."

## Equity Considerations

In considering such a recommendation, which was derived rather mechanically from the application of the concept of marginal productivity, the budgetmaker will undoubtedly want to think about the moral and social issues involved. After all, the ratio of "cures" per dollar may be declining, but the number of cures is still rising. And that, given the destructive consequences of alcoholism, is worth supporting.

Questions of social and economic equity intrude into every budget, testing the moral probity of its makers. Politics being what it is, public budgets tend to reflect the interests of the powerful. Therefore, budgetmakers have a duty to support allocations which protect rights and correct wrongs, grounding their recommendations in moral considerations.

## Estimating Benefits

Support for "equity" allocations often depends on the budgetmakers' ability to broaden the concept of benefits, showing net returns to those who finance, as well as to those who are to enjoy, the service in question. The estimation of benefits is difficult, but not impossible. To apply investment criteria, as suggested, budgetmakers must develop and maintain a suitable data base. Experts on the subject agree that the public's willingness to pay—as distinguished from its ability to pay—is the surest index of benefit. This data can be gleaned from private market prices for services analogous to public services (book prices versus library unit costs of circulation; private recreation prices—bowling, movies, skiing, etc.—matched against public-recreation unit costs; and so on).

Establishing service charges and polling users of public services on their willingness to pay are two additional ways to garner data on benefits. Cost avoidance, or savings, ascribed to investments is also legitimately included in benefit calculations. Furthermore, benefits can be described as positive (+ but ?), or negative (- but ?) if the tendency is known but the benefits cannot be accurately estimated. See Exhibit 5 on p. 27 for an example of the use of this technique.

Remember, every public budget is presumed by its supporters to yield benefits equal to, or exceeding, its cost. This idea can be expressed in the following way:

$$\frac{\text{Benefits}}{\text{Investment}} \geq 1 + r$$

where $r$ is the opportunity cost of the investment, expressed as the prevailing rate of interest, in percent. For example, assuming an interest rate of 5 percent, a budget proposal of $100,000 must produce ascribed benefits that equal or exceed $105,000.

Proving that budget proposals meet this basic "admissibility" criterion is, in itself, a major burden for budgetmakers, to say nothing of the analytical burdens which confront them when they try to apply investment criteria to evaluate the relative merits of a spectrum of proposals.

## Weighting-and-Scoring Models

Budgetmakers who despair of applying investment criteria often use weighting-and-scoring models to illuminate the comparative worth of competitive proposals. The simplest and most popular weighting scheme calls for priority ranking by ordinal designations (i.e., first, second, third, etc.) of a group of investment proposals. This procedure is the key feature of zero-base budgeting. Ordinal ranking may be assigned by individuals or by groups using agreed-upon criteria and decision rules. Proposals may also be sorted into broad-priority categories, such as high, medium, and low, and then given an ordinal rank within the assigned class.

Scoring models can also help budgetmakers assign priorities. Points are given to each proposal by reference to a table of values. For example, the leaders of a local government establish the relative importance of its functions by assigning ordinal rankings, such as public safety (1), public health (2), and public education (3). Another scale is established for the leading attributes of each proposal, according to a scheme of criteria, such as legally prescribed (1), increases tax base (2), and reduces unit cost (3). See Exhibit 12 for an example of the resulting matrix.

In weighting and scoring, budgetmakers assign numbers to the proposals under consideration. The numbers are drawn from two or more rank-ordered lists, such as the two shown in Exhibit 12. This matrix has a list of functional priorities, ranked first, second, and so on, running down the left side, and a list of allocation criteria, ranked zero, first, second, and so on, running along the top. Note that a zero value is assigned to the "legally prescribed" category, and any proposal so described is automatically given the highest rank, regardless of its place on the list of functional priorities. The numbers are then multiplied to yield a priority ranking for each proposal. For example,

**EXHIBIT 12. A Weighting-and-Scoring Model**

|  |  | *Legally Prescribed* | *Increases Tax Base* | *Reduces Unit Cost* | *Standard Service* | *Service Expansion* |
|---|---|---|---|---|---|---|
| **Functional Priorities** |  | 0 | 1 | 2 | 3 | 4 |
| *Public safety* | 1 | 0 | 1 | 2 | 3 | 4 |
| *Public health* | 2 | 0 | 2 | 4 | 6 | 8 |
| *Public education* | 3 | 0 | 3 | 6 | 9 | 12 |
| *Civic/cultural* | 4 | 0 | 4 | 8 | 12 | 16 |
| *Public convenience* | 5 | 0 | 5 | 10 | 15 | 20 |

Allocation Criteria

using the matrix shown in Exhibit 12, a proposal to correct a hazardous street condition would be assigned a "1" from the list of functional priorities, and a "4" from the list of allocation criteria because it is a new project. Multiplying these two figures yields a product of 4. The proposal is then assigned to priority group 4.

Obviously, weighting-and-scoring models organize—rather than eliminate—the subjective judgments of those involved in the budget process. This can be a major benefit. Indeed, budgetmakers who use weighting-and-scoring models report that beneficial results flow from the establishment of the matrix itself, because it forces budget participants to clarify and objectify their values.

# UNIT 5
# Budget Formulation

## FORMAT SPECIFICATIONS

As pointed out in Unit 4, budgets presumably have production functions, which are described by the equation, $y = f(x)$. Given this, it can be seen that budgets should be formulated in ways which illuminate the variables embraced by the equation. What goods are to be produced, and why? Who needs them, and for how long? Are production techniques justified? Are options available? Such questions must govern the formulation of budgets, and therefore, they dictate the format for budget requests.

Accordingly, a proper budget request should incorporate a multiyear perspective and a five-part commentary which covers the following topics:

- problem definition and goal(s)
- target population
- performance criteria
- preferred solution: impacts and benefits
- rejected alternative

This format is designed to provoke broad thinking. It requires budget-makers to organize information and to describe the leading ideas

**Issue-Paper Structure**

supporting a proposal to spend public funds. A budget proposal prepared in this format is called a *program memorandum* or an *issue paper*.

Now study Exhibit 13, a sample program memo dealing with a proposed budget for health services delivered in homes rather than institutions. Note that the structure of the memo follows the specifications outlined previously. These specifications help budgetmakers to apply logic and mathematical techniques to the facts of particular cases, thus fostering the diagnosis and analysis of (1) problems and/or issues, (2) controlling variables which must be changed to "solve" or "resolve" issues, (3) attainable goals, (4) target population characteristics, and (5) the criteria taken into consideration in making budgetary decisions.

The structure of an issue paper imposes a logical framework on the development of proposals to allocate public funds. A preferred solution, for example, must be logically related to a previously stipulated problem and defined in terms of the controlling variables. It must also be related to the stated characteristics of the target population and to the criteria advanced to justify the selected production technique. Because the parts of an issue paper are so interrelated, its composition is governed by rather strict logic. Inconsistency, non sequiturs, and other lapses of logic almost always indicate diagnostic or analytical weaknesses, or both.

**Instructions**

This unit is organized around an exercise on animal control in the fictional city of Centerville. The facts of the case are presented first, followed by a set of budget formulation guidelines.

Study the animal-control exercise, and then consult the guidelines for assistance in thinking through the problem. Note that the guidelines supply helpful hints concerning the exercise. In addition, they provide examples of how to apply issue-paper thinking to other problems—in this instance, nutrition for the elderly. For guidance on the layout of your issue paper, refer to Exhibit 13.

## ANIMAL CONTROL IN CENTERVILLE: AN EXERCISE IN BUDGET FORMULATION

**The Setting**

The city of Centerville, population 54,600 and growing, relies on the privately owned ABC Kennels for the impoundment of stray animals. This shelter is located in south Centerville, 10 miles from the population center of the city, where the animal warden and a

EXHIBIT 13. A Sample Program Memo

---

**PROGRAM MEMO**

To: Chief Executive

From: Director of Health

Subject: Home Care

Date: 00/00/00

| Expenditures | Budget Year 1 | Budget Year 2 | Budget Year 3 | Budget Year 4 | Budget Year 5 |
|---|---|---|---|---|---|
| Home care | $70,000 | $75,000 | $80,000 | $85,000 | $90,000 |

| Financing Plan | Budget Year 1 | Budget Year 2 | Budget Year 3 | Budget Year 4 | Budget Year 5 |
|---|---|---|---|---|---|
| Private grant   | $ 7,000  | $ 7,500  | $ 7,200  | $ 6,600  | $ 6,000  |
| Service charges | 61,600   | 67,200   | 72,800   | 78,400   | 84,000   |
| Property taxes  | 1,400    | 300      |          |          |          |
|                 | $70,000  | $75,000  | $80,000  | $85,000  | $90,000  |

*PROBLEM DEFINITION AND GOAL.* As originally specified in our "issue paper" last year, the steadily rising cost of institutional care for stroke and fracture victims, and the ensuing financial drain on victim, family, and, in welfare cases, society, were defined as a problem requiring public action. Started last year as an efficient, less costly alternative to institutionalized care, a home care team, on contract from the ABC Rehabilitation Center, can be expected to deliver coordinated therapeutic services to an estimated 220 persons in the next fiscal year, up 20 from the current-year estimate of 200. A 5-year forecast follows:

| Performance Data | Cases | Unit Cost |
|---|---|---|
| Current year   | 200 | $325 |
| Budget year 1  | 220 | 318  |
| Budget year 2  | 240 | 313  |
| Budget year 3  | 260 | 308  |
| Budget year 4  | 280 | 304  |
| Budget year 5  | 300 | 300  |

As you will recall, this service got started with a pledge from the XYZ Foundation to support the service to at least the 10 percent level. As noted in the multiyear plan, an expected increase in case load reduces unit costs to a point where the foundation grant decreases to 6.7 percent, and the taxpayer subsidy disappears. As the break-even point for full self-financing is 500 cases, elimination of Foundation support will

---

*From Edward A. Lehan, *Simplified Governmental Budgeting* (Chicago: Municipal Finance Officers Association, 1981), pp. 40–41. Reprinted with permission.

**EXHIBIT 13 (cont.)**

Home Care Program Memo
Page 2

not occur in the coming 5-year period, unless service charges are increased beyond the $280 average for each case. This alternative will be discussed in the last part of this memo.

*TARGET POPULATION.* Stroke and fracture victims predominate among the referrals from doctors and area hospitals. We also provide service to chronically ill persons with the object of either making them comfortable, or reducing their dependency. With stroke and fracture victims, our physical and speech therapists aim at self-care, and beyond that, economic productivity. Our estimates of case-load growth are based on (1) increased awareness of our service, (2) projections of higher incidence of strokes, and (3) the drive of hospitals to reduce the length of stays.

*PERFORMANCE CRITERIA.* Cost avoidance is the primary measure of success. As noted below, in the cross-classification of home care costs and benefits, the net benefits are calculated at $184,000 in the coming year, a 263% return on our investment. In addition, note that a small portion of this gain is expected to derive from an earlier return of patients to economic productivity, a secondary measure of program success.

*PREFERRED SOLUTION: IMPACTS AND BENEFITS.* The concept of this program, delivery of therapeutic services in the home, will require an investment of $70,000 next year. The following exhibit cross-classifies this investment and its ascribed benefits by three impact categories:

|  | *Reducing Personal Dependency* | *Reducing Economic Dependency* | *General Welfare* |
|---|---|---|---|
| **COSTS** | | | |
| Number of cases | 70 | 60 | 90 |
| Case cost | $20,950 | $28,800 | $20,250 |
| **BENEFITS** | | | |
| Unneeded institutional care | $60,000 | $50,000 | $90,000 |
| Unneeded nursing care | 24,000 | | |
| Patient productivity | | 30,000 | |
| | $84,000 | $80,000 | $90,000 |

(IMPACTS)

Each of the 220 cases expected next year has been classified according to its potential. In 70 cases, costing $20,950, the therapeutic effort is aimed at improving the patient's capability for self-care, eliminating an estimated 600 days of institutionalized care @ $100, or $60,000, and 600 days of home nursing care @ $40, or $24,000. Benefits will exceed costs by $63,050.

EXHIBIT 13 (cont.)

Home Care Program Memo
Page 3

In 60 cases, costing $28,800, the patient has the potential to work again. Home care will eliminate 500 days of institutional care @ $100, or $50,000, and, in addition, may claim a certain amount of economic impact by promoting a more rapid recovery in the home, in contrast to the rate of recovery experienced in an institution. Ten working days per patient @ $50 is regarded as a fair estimate of the economic gain due to home care. Total estimated benefits of $80,000 exceed costs by $51,200.

In 90 cases, costing $20,250, the aim is to make the patient as comfortable as possible. No significant gains in either self-care or economic productivity are expected. In these cases, home care eliminates an estimated 900 days of hospital or convalescent care @ $100, or $90,000, with this benefit exceeding costs by $69,750.

In total, we can assign savings or benefits worth $254,000 to home care during the coming fiscal year, an amount exceeding costs by $184,000.

*REJECTED ALTERNATIVES.* This program is an alternative to institutional care and to clinic-based therapy. Therefore, it is workable as long as its costs compare favorably with the costs of institutionalization. We are estimating costs of $70,000 in the coming fiscal year. This is $130,000 less than the estimated cost of $200,000 which 220 patients would probably incur if institutionalized. Thus, we are predicting a net gain on this level of comparison alone. Other savings and economic benefits (harder to estimate and verify) shown in the matrix only strengthen the case for the home care alternative.

We are reluctant to recommend an increase in our service charge, $20 per visit, until we have concurrence from the health insurance industry. To do otherwise would only increase the burden on our patients, many of whom are hardship cases. With the small taxpayer subsidy being phased out completely in future year 3 as the number of cases rises (lowering unit costs), and with the continued support of the XYZ Foundation assured, the only reason we can see for raising rates would be inflationary pressures on our costs.

# EXHIBIT 14. Animal-Control Performance Data

|  | Past Year 3 | Past Year 2 | Past Year 1 | ESTIMATES This Year | Next Year |
|---|---|---|---|---|---|
| Complaints | 3,500 | 3,600 | 3,800 | 4,100 | 4,500 |
| Licensed dogs | 1,350 | 1,450 | 1,550 | 1,650 | 1,750 |
| Impoundments | 550 | 620 | 680 | 730 | 770 |
| Impoundment cost | $16,620 | $17,450 | $18,325 | $19,240 | $20,200 |
| Unit cost | $30.22 | $28.15 | $26.95 | $26.36 | $26.23 |

part-time assistant have their headquarters. This distance and its costs to the city have become an issue in Centerville.

Exhibit 14 shows that the number of complaints (mainly about roaming dogs) has been rising annually at an *increasing* rate, the number of licensed dogs has been increasing at a *constant* rate, and the number of impoundments has been increasing at a *declining* rate.

The contract with ABC Kennels calls for the city to pay $2.00 daily for each impounded animal. Owners redeeming animals must reimburse the city for this cost, as well as pay a service charge of $10.00. Currently, 50 percent of the impounded animals are redeemed after an average stay of 2 days. Revenue from this source is estimated to be $5,110 this year. The current-year budget, organized in a commodity or line-item format, is shown in Exhibit 15.

# EXHIBIT 15. Current-Year Animal-Control Budget

|  | Estimate |
|---|---|
| Regular payroll (2,080 hours @ $4.50) | $ 9,360 |
| Overtime payments (125 hours @ $6.75) | 845 |
| Part-time payroll (832 hours @ $3.00) | 2,495 |
| Benefits (20%) | 1,870 |
| General administration | 2,000 |
| Transportation (30,900 miles @ $0.20) | 6,180 |
| Boarding fees (730 dogs, 4.5 days @ $2.00) | 6,570 |
| Animal disposal (365 dogs @ $5.00) | 1,825 |
|  | $31,145 |

The wardens currently spend an estimated 10 hours weekly in shelter-related trips, at an average hourly cost of $4.80 ($2,495 annually) in wages and benefits and $0.20 per mile in vehicle costs ($2,080 annually).

Assuming continuing growth in the animal-control work load, Centerville faces higher budgets for this activity next year and in the years ahead. Many officials and citizens believe that it is time to redefine the animal-control problem, including its goals and procedures. As a result, they favor the construction of a shelter on a privately owned, half-acre site, adjacent to the public safety center, a move long advocated by the Centerville Humane Association.

The association recommends a 20-pen shelter, complete with runs, cages for cats and other animals, a euthanasia chamber, a crematorium, a food storage and preparation area, a restroom, and a small office. The estimated cost, $50,000, includes land acquisition. The warden points out that the proposed shelter will increase public convenience and reduce both city-employee and citizen travel time and costs. In the current year, citizens will spend an estimated 365 hours and log 7,300 miles redeeming their dogs. Valuing citizen time at $5.00 per hour and mileage at $0.20 per mile, the warden estimates current-year citizen travel costs at $3,285.

Critics of the proposal to build a new shelter point out that it serves the interests of dog owners who permit their pets to run without restraint. Construction of a shelter, they say, represents a failure to achieve the public interest, which is the elimination of strays, not their impoundment at public expense. The alternative to shelter construction is regulation.

A leash law, steeper fines, higher service charges and license fees, and an animal contraception campaign are all alternatives which might achieve the goals of the animal-control function better than shelter construction and operation, which tends, according to its critics, to be counterproductive.

## The Warden's Dilemma

The warden acknowledges that if implemented, these regulatory alternatives would eliminate the need for a new shelter. However, based on past performance, the warden believes that "politics" will block any hope for a regulatory solution, thus leaving the warden little choice but to support the less desirable alternative of shelter construction. Based on a preliminary analysis, the warden believes that, given little or no change in regulatory policies, a properly sited in-city pound would reduce overall social costs. Reluctantly, the warden recommends that $50,000 for pound construction be added to the current-year estimate, resulting in a budget request of $81,145.

**Your Assignment**

Imagine yourself as the animal warden in the city of Centerville. Think through the problem facing the warden, and prepare an issue paper for the consideration of your superiors. Recall that the warden weighed the following three alternatives, rejecting the first two:

- continue the current practice
- experiment with a regulatory solution
- construct a new shelter

You are free to define the situation and its solution as you see fit, taking care to employ unit measures, investment returns, or both, to justify your recommendation. The program memo form provided in Exhibit 16 incorporates a section for listing the costs of shelter construction. In order to assist you, these construction costs have been estimated and listed on the form.

Exhibit 17 will also help you in your analysis of the construction alternative. The amortization and first-year interest charges have been determined and listed, leaving all other decisions to you. Remember, in order to judge its investment worthiness, you must establish an admissibility criterion—that is, the threshold opportunity cost of the proposed new shelter. See Unit 4 to refresh your memory on this point.

The three alternatives will probably have different utilities, measured in terms of complaints, licensed dogs, fees, impoundments, damage to persons and property, and so on. Thus, they will have different positions on any marginal utility curves you may construct in the course of your analysis. In addition, the line-item format of the current budget should be reclassified to express your programmatic intentions.

**EXHIBIT 16. Program Memo: Proposed Budget for Animal Control**

## PROGRAM MEMO

To: Police Chief

From: Animal Warden

Subject: Proposed Budget for Animal Control          Date:

| Expenditures | Budget Year 1 | Budget Year 2 | Budget Year 3 | Budget Year 4 | Budget Year 5 |
|---|---|---|---|---|---|
|  |  |  |  |  |  |

| Financing Plan | Budget Year 1 | Budget Year 2 | Budget Year 3 | Budget Year 4 | Budget Year 5 |
|---|---|---|---|---|---|
|  |  |  |  |  |  |

```
        Shelter Construction Costs

Design                          $ 3,000
Land acquisition                  4,000
Demolition
Site improvement                  1,000
Construction                     25,000
Landscaping                       1,000
Furniture/equipment              10,000
Miscellaneous                     1,000
Contingency                       5,000
                                $50,000
```

*PROBLEM DEFINITION AND GOAL:*

EXHIBIT 17. Cost Analysis Worksheet: Shelter Construction

|  | Current Costs | Costs with New Shelter | + or (−) |
|---|---|---|---|
| ABC boarding and disposal fees | $ 8,395 | $ 0 | $8,395 (−) |
| Shelter operation @ $?/day | 0 | _____ | _____ |
| Warden's travel @ $0.20/mile | 2,080 | _____ | _____ |
| Warden's time @ $4.80/hour | 2,495 | _____ | _____ |
| Citizens' travel @ $0.20/mile | 1,460 | _____ | _____ |
| Citizens' time @ $5/hour | 1,825 | _____ | _____ |
| Amortization @ cost/20 years | 0 | 2,500 | 2,500 |
| First-year interest @ 5% | 0 | 2,500 | 2,500 |
| Taxes on 0.5 acre | ( 100) | 0 | 100 |
| Service charges | ( 5,110) | _____ | _____ |
|  | $11,245 | $_____ | $_____ |

# BUDGET FORMULATION GUIDELINES*

The guidelines which follow divide the budget formulation task into two phases: (1) diagnosis and (2) analysis of alternatives. Generally, the time devoted to the diagnostic phase far exceeds the time required for the weighing of alternatives. Some experienced budget-makers report that the ratio of diagnostic to analytical time should be about four to one, indicating the critical importance of a correct assessment of the problem to be addressed by the allocation of public funds.

**Diagnostic Focus**

## DIAGNOSIS: THE PRELIMINARY WORK

Begin by employing broad survey techniques. Review pertinent data in files and documents, and search the formal literature. Where appropriate, conduct field inspections. Finally, consult with people who can offer insight and advice.

**Loosen Up Your Thinking**

These steps will help you define the scope of the problem, the relative significance of the data at hand, and the data which must be assembled. In addition, the steps will also assist you in mastering the special nomenclature of the science or techniques involved in the program situation.

Remember, experienced analysts agree that conventional or obvious statements about public problems should be regarded with suspicion, lest administrators and policymakers be led to dwell on symptoms, or worse, on erroneous questions.

**Conventional Problem Statements May Mislead**

Suppose the problem concerns the nutrition of the elderly portion of the population. In this case, do not take at face value any of the assumptions which might be put forward as problem definitions, such as the assumed impact of nutrition on health, the listing of personal limitations or barriers preventing the elderly from enjoying good diets, and the presumed failure of institutions to meet the needs of the elderly.

In the animal-control case, the warden tends to define the problem in rather logistical terms: efficient impoundment is the problem,

---

*These guidelines incorporate material appearing in Edward A. Lehan, *Simplified Governmental Budgeting* (Chicago: Municipal Finance Officers Association, 1981), pp. 40-45. Reprinted with permission.

and a new, better-located pound is the solution. The Centerville Humane Association supports this definition on compassionate grounds. Both the warden and the association resist a broader definition dealing with the causes of the animal-control problem.

**Action Research**

The diagnosis is to be oriented toward action, or performance, not knowledge for its own sake. As decision-related research, the problem definition must be sufficiently broad to identify the controlling variables, establish objectives, and specify performance criteria. Referring again to the nutrition of the elderly, for example, the isolation of the elderly may be identified as the critical element in the situation—that is, the factor which, if altered, would decisively affect the nutritional status of the elderly. The identification of isolation as a controlling variable would have important implications, because the choice of goals, the selection of the target population, and the performance criteria would then logically relate to it.

In the animal-control case, the warden identifies official and citizen logistics as the controlling variable and suggests that a budget attacking this variable will produce a better impoundment situation. In focusing on official and citizen travel problems and costs, the warden foregoes an attack on another possible controlling variable, animal-owner motivation. If owner motivation can be positively influenced, the animal-nuisance situation could be altered at its roots, reducing impoundments—and the need for a new pound—in the bargain. Thus, due to its impact on behavior, licensing also merits consideration as a controlling variable.

**The Achilles' Heel of Policy**

Study the demographic and logistical characteristics of the situation. *Who, what, when, where,* and *how* questions deeply intrude into all aspects of public programming. (Remember: implementation is the Achilles' heel of policy!) Regarding the nutrition of the elderly, techniques of statistical inference might be used to gain an understanding of how geographical and population characteristics, such as poverty and density, interact. If, for example, the distributions of elderly poverty and elderly density are not congruent, what are the implications for service delivery?

In the animal-control case, nuisances and the resulting complaints may not be randomly distributed. Instead, the situation may involve many chronic offenders and equally chronic complainers.

## CONCLUDING THE DIAGNOSTIC PHASE

Before the analysis of alternatives is begun, the results of the diagnostic phase must be put in writing.

**Problem Definition and Goal**

First, compose a problem definition and a resulting goal statement. As a rule, avoid completely verbal goal statements, such as, "Improve the nutrition of the elderly." Try instead to frame a goal statement in numerical terms, such as "Reduce the number of elderly citizens with anemia from _____ to _____ in _____ months."

In the animal-control case, if licensing is chosen as the critical factor, one could frame the following goal statement: "Increase the number of licensed animals from an estimated 1,650 in the current year to 1,750 next year." This goal could also be stated in terms of proportions: "Increase the percentage of licensed animals from an estimated 50 percent in the current year to 53 percent next year."

In addition, setting goals in a numerical way tends to ensure that chosen goals are practical and measurable. A goal, to be practical, must be attainable in a specific time. Remember, success in implementation is directly related to choosing goals which are practical—that is, attainable. Furthermore, it is easier to set milestones or performance checkpoints, which are an essential part of a work plan, if the chosen goal is measurable.

**Target Population**

Next, describe the target population. Every public program has a clientele, willing or not. An accurate description of the target population lends precision to the goal statement and makes it possible for an analysis of impacts and benefits to begin. Target groups comprise those individuals, organized or not, perhaps even unborn, who are to be affected by the expenditures outlined in the multiyear financial projection.

Who comprises the target population of Centerville's animal-control program? Those owning animals? Those owners permitting animal nuisances? Or those nonowners who benefit from the regulatory and service procedures?

Because the description of impacts and benefits depends on a good description of program clientele, one should be as accurate as possible in identifying the target population. Of course, more precision than the situation allows is not expected. For example, a public-works director, charged with keeping the public way passable and safe, will not find it easy to accurately specify the number or characteristics of persons benefiting from expenditures for street maintenance, lighting, snow removal, and so on. Often, approximations must suffice. A public-works director can develop data which can stand as a substitute for direct data on the target population. Information on traffic and its volume, speed, and direction might substitute very nicely for people, particularly if such data are classified by type of street (e.g., local, connector, arterial) and are linked to accident and street-crime information.

**Performance Criteria**

Once you have produced a tentative goal statement and described the potential target population, outline the performance criteria. Performance criteria include the leading ideas, the causal relationships, the assumptions, and the standards which influence the size, shape, and direction of a proposed program. Minimum daily nutritional requirements for the elderly is an example of a standard which, if applied, would have an important impact on program design. Protecting the privacy and enhancing the independence of the target population might also be considered in testing alternative ways of improving elderly nutrition.

Similarly, the impoundment standards of the Centerville Humane Association will probably play an important role in the animal-control case, if the jurisdiction adopts a budget for a new pound.

Causal relationships, or correlations, are particularly important. For example, in the case of elderly nutrition, it might be hypothesized that health (defined in terms of longer life and reduced institutionalization) is partially dependent on nutrition, thus making nutrition a controlling variable which can be manipulated in desirable ways by various strategies. Remember, correlations, or causal relationships, provide the firmest foundations for program planning and implementation.

In the animal-control case, one might study the correlation between licensing and animal-owner responsibility. If most nuisances are caused by nonlicensed animals, a direct attack on delinquent owners through a census, steep fines, and so on, might be a worthy alternative to constructing a shelter or increasing staff hours to cope with increasing complaints.

## ANALYTICAL PHASE: THE STUDY OF ALTERNATIVES

Determining program approaches which give some promise of achieving the goals, with minimum side effects, is the next task. Proper comparison of the impacts and benefits of the respective alternatives should yield a preferred course of action. This preferred alternative should produce the highest net return to society. Moreover, the benefit ascribed to the preferred alternative should equal or exceed its estimated cost.

In addition to recommending "no action at all," the range of alternatives in the elderly-nutrition case might include common meals, home-delivered meals, homemaker services, supervised shopping, income supplements, and nutrition instruction. Note that each alternative chosen for analysis must be directly related to the problem definition and goals, target population, and performance criteria. Otherwise, the resulting issue paper will lack logical coherence. For example, if, in the problem definition, isolation is identified as a critical factor (or controlling variable) having powerful effects on nutrition, then the relative utility of socialization or housing programs aimed at the isolation of the elderly must be assessed, under the assumption that the reduction of isolation will also reduce malnutrition as a desirable by-product. On the other hand, given the problem definition, one would not put much analytical effort into the study of income supplements, as such payments would have little or no impact on isolation, the controlling variable.

In the animal-control case, depending on one's choice of controlling variable(s), the alternatives might include increased staffing, construction of a new pound, a licensing drive, an animal census, an education campaign, a leash law, steep fines, higher service charges, and sterilization services.

## Impacts and Benefits

One must exercise imagination and ingenuity in devising ways to compare the impacts and benefits of alternatives. In general, data on costs are much easier to assemble than data on benefits. Use the best sources available. Consult the literature for help in applying various analytical techniques, such as cost-effectiveness and benefit-cost, which might help in the comparison of alternatives.

Obviously, attempts to compare alternatives by means of analytical techniques require that any presumed linkages between the variables be specified. For example, in the elderly-nutrition problem, the presumed linkage between nutrition and health can be explored by assessing the relative efficiency of alternative program approaches, such as home-delivered meals and congregate living, in reducing the number of days lost to death and disability by the target population. By assigning a dollar value to each day of life and to the daily cost of institutional care, it is then possible to use benefit-cost comparisons to determine which alternative produces the highest net return.

Given the obvious difficulties of specifying the linkage of possible program approaches to elderly nutrition and the impact of nutrition on health, many students of this problem recommend an action-research experiment in programming, rather than a definitive program recommendation. By this means, various alternatives can be tested with representative populations, measuring results of each against the performance of the total elderly population.

In the animal-control case, a benefits schedule might well include personal injury, property damage, public convenience, and cost avoidance. In searching for the benefits of the animal-control program, one should not overlook the considerable value of the impoundment procedure to those whose pets inadvertently stray away. After all, half of the animals impounded in Centerville are redeemed.

Remember, the means of implementation must be built up in the course of analysis. Alternatives which look good analytically may not look practical to implementers. Involving potential implementers in the analysis of alternatives is a good way to avoid wasting time and resources on the study of unrealistic approaches.

## Multiyear Projections

A budget request should include a multiyear projection of program costs and a financing plan (i.e., taxes, grants, service charges, and so on). This helps reviewers and policymakers to get an idea of the future implications of adopting the alternative preferred by the budgetmaker. In addition, each year's financing plan should provide funds which equal or exceed the proposed expenditures.

## Rejected Alternatives

A budget request should conclude with a concise commentary on the rejected alternatives. Such a commentary forces the author(s) of a proposal to maintain consistent criteria for the examination of all options. Furthermore, it provides reviewers and policymakers with a broad context, thus helping to inspire confidence in a proposal as a thoughtful response to a carefully considered problem.

# UNIT 6
# Budget Adoption

## A GENERIC PROCESS

Legally, a budget is adopted when competent authorities (usually legislatures) review and accept estimates by enacting appropriations. However, such authorities have no monopoly on adoption. Rather, adoption happens at every level of budgeting. Department heads review and adopt the estimates of subordinates, passing them along as their own. Budget officers and chief executives do the same.
In formulating and adopting a budget, budgetmakers express allocation criteria. Thus far, we have discussed the influence of allocation criteria in budget formulation. In this unit, we will explore the application of criteria in the process of budget adoption.

When budgetmakers review estimates formulated by others, they do so selectively. As a rule, they concentrate on new initiatives or significant changes in established patterns. Furthermore, big items attract more interest than do small ones. When making adjustments—usually reductions—in a scheme of estimates, budget reviewers often focus on discretionary items and expenditures which can be put off, such as equipment purchases and maintenance projects.
In addition, salary allotments, particularly those supporting administrative personnel, usually enjoy more favor than do operating ex-

**Selective Approach Favored**

penses. In the exercise which follows, will your decisions reveal similar considerations?

**THE EXERCISE**

Exhibit 18 presents four proposals: code enforcement and home care, both drawn from Unit 2; alcoholic treatment drawn from Unit 3; and animal control, drawn from Unit 5. Complete with an integrated financing plan, these proposals are grouped together in a single summary to give us a four-function budget.

# EXHIBIT 18. Budget Adoption Worksheet

|  | This Year | Proposed Budget | Adopted Budget |
|---|---|---|---|
| *Investments* | | | |
| Code enforcement | $ 118,250 | $ 139,420 | $_____ |
| Home care | 65,000 | 70,000 | _____ |
| Alcoholic treatment | 100,000 | 100,000 | _____ |
| Animal control | 31,145 | 81,145 | _____ |
|  | $ 314,395 | $ 390,565 | |
| *Financing Plan* | | | |
| Code enforcement fees | $ 86,750 | $ 93,250 | $_____ |
| Private grant | 6,500 | 7,000 | _____ |
| Home-care service charges | 56,000 | 61,600 | _____ |
| Animal-control service charges | 5,110 | 5,390 | _____ |
| Property taxes | 166,770 | 223,325 | _____ |
| Shelter construction loan | | | _____ |
| Surplus | $ 321,130 | $ 390,565 | |
| *Financial Data* | | | |
| Assessed property value (AV) | $3,369,100 | $3,706,010 | $3,706,010 |
| Tax rate per $1,000 of AV | 50.00 | 63.43 | _____ |
| Code enforcement fee per permit | 50.00 | 50.00 | _____ |
| Home-care charge per visit[a] | 20.00 | 20.00 | _____ |
| Animal impoundment fee per day | 2.00 | 2.00 | _____ |
| Impoundment charge per case | 10.00 | 10.00 | _____ |

[a] Average of 14 visits per case.

Imagine yourself as a legislator preparing for a vote on this recommended budget. In reviewing the proposed budget, you are expected to rely on the analytical data associated with each proposal. Register your decisions on both investments and the financing plan on the worksheet in the adopted budget column. The only figure that you cannot change is the assessed value of taxable property.

**Financing Issues**

As noted in the financial data section of the worksheet, this four-function budget of $390,565 requires a tax rate of $63.43 per $1,000 of the assessed value of taxable property, up significantly from the $50.00 tax rate of the current year. This occurs despite a 10 percent increase in assessed values.

The tax rate is calculated as follows:

$$\frac{\text{Tax levy}}{\text{Assessments}} = \text{Tax rate}$$

In this case, the tax levy of $235,079 is divided by the assessments of $3,706,010, yielding a tax rate of 0.06343. This figure is then multiplied by $1,000 to produce the more easily understood figure of $63.43 per $1,000. (In many jurisdictions, this figure would be identified as 63.43 mills. A *mill* is one thousandth of a dollar.) Note that the tax receipt of $223,325 listed in the proposed budget is only 95 percent of the tax levy, reflecting an allowance for uncollected taxes.

In the current year, tax receipts of $166,770 are estimated at 99 percent of the current year's tax levy. Because only 95 percent of this levy was listed in the original budget, the improved collection rate produces an estimated current-year surplus of $6,735, which has not been included as a revenue in the proposed budget. You may include it if you wish. You may also want to increase the tax-collection ratio of 95 percent to a higher percentage, reflecting the experience of the current year. This will reduce the tax rate.

All fees and service charges remain unchanged. However, you may want to revise the schedule of fees and charges according to your vision of proper public policy and taxpayer equity. If the schedule is increased, it will tend to reduce taxes.

The animal-control budget includes an allotment of $50,000 to construct a shelter. The financing plan calls for this investment to be funded by property taxes. Of course, all or part of the investment could be financed by a loan. Should you adopt this project, a financing option is open to you. Any part of the investment that is financed by borrowing will reduce its initial impact on taxes by spreading loan payments over a period of years.

**Investment Issues**

In considering the four investment proposals, try to find a basis for comparing their worth. First, apply the investment criterion by constructing a formal comparison of investment returns. As suggested in Unit 1, such a comparison organizes the available data on benefits and promotes the search for additional data. Exhibit 19 provides a worksheet for the formal comparison of the four proposals, with the gross benefits of home care inserted. Based on your work on the animal-control problem, you should be able to ascribe a reasonable estimate of benefit for your recommended investment. In the alcoholic-treatment case, you should be able to ascribe benefits based on published studies of the social and economic consequences of addiction.

The benefits of the code enforcement investment—that is, safe, stable structures—are undoubtedly large, but they are difficult, perhaps impossible, to determine to anyone's satisfaction. Surely, that investment, even though it may be technically weak at its margin because of the productivity decline, meets the admissibility criterion. As willingness to pay is the best indicator of benefit, the permit fee might be examined in relation to the benefit conferred, raising the fees to the level of the admissibility criterion: that is, cost plus a reasonable rate of interest.

Next, assess these proposals in terms of their marginal productivity. The code enforcement budget is up significantly. But, as you will recall, an examination of its performance data raises some questions. The home-care budget is also up, but shows increasing effectiveness and decreasing unit costs. As already indicated, the proposed increase in the animal-control budget supports a $50,000 investment in a new animal shelter. Depending on your analysis of shelter benefits, this investment may or may not produce increasing productivity. In any case, the marginal return on the new shelter will probably not match the increasing benefits ascribed to home care. Finally, the alcoholic-treatment budget, in line with current-year experience, exhibits declining marginal productivity.

**Balance Your Budget**

Enter your decisions about these four investments and the associated finances in the adopted budget column of Exhibit 18. Be sure that your budget balances—that is, that revenues equal expenditures.

**Make Notes**

As you make your decisions, clarify your thinking by jotting down notes. This will help you prepare for the final exercise of this workbook, an assessment essay on the question, What is good budgeting?

**EXHIBIT 19. Investment Return Comparison**

| Cost Centers | Gross Benefits | (−) | Investment | = | Net Benefits | Investment Return |
|---|---|---|---|---|---|---|
| Code enforcement | $ _____ | | $139,420 | | $ _____ | _____ |
| Home care | 249,000 | | 70,000 | | 179,000 | 256% |
| Alcoholic treatment | _____ | | 10,000 | | _____ | _____ |
| Animal control | _____ | | _____ | | _____ | _____ |

# Assessment Essay

**SUMMING UP**

Before you started this workbook, you were asked to crystallize your thinking about budgeting in a benchmark essay. Now that you have completed your study, it is appropriate that you compose another brief essay. Write it without referring to the earlier essay; then compare the two. This comparison will show you what you have learned by using this workbook.

Use p. 89 to record your thinking on the question, What is good budgeting?

# What Is Good Budgeting?

# GLOSSARY

**ALLOTMENT**
An appropriation segment. Appropriations are often subdivided and allotted piecemeal by executive authorities in order to achieve specific purposes in limited periods of time.

**APPROPRIATION**
The limited right to spend. By formally assigning scarce resources, policymakers appropriate sums for specific purposes and times. In certain cases, such as capital investments, appropriations may not specify time limits.

**BUDGET**
A distribution of scarce resources.

**BUDGET DOCUMENT**
A printed compilation of appropriation and revenue data. Although budget documents vary in content, they usually include historical expenditure and revenue information; appropriation titles, sums, and associated revenue estimates; and supporting tabular and narrative documentation.

**CAPITAL OUTLAY**
An acquisition of fixed assets. As an object classification, capital outlay is applied to expenditures for land, buildings, machinery, equipment, and so on.

**COMMODITY FORMAT**
See *Line-Item Budget*.

**COST CENTER**
An aggregation of expense. As building blocks, cost-center titles are used to identify and sum costs for comparison with appropriation, allotment, and performance data.

## CROSS-CLASSIFICATION

The assignment of an expenditure or revenue to more than one classification. Cross-classification is also known as a "crosswalk" in the literature of the planning/programming/budgeting system (PPBS).

## DIMINISHING RETURNS

An axiom of economic thought. When applied to budgeting, it suggests that increases in expenditure for any given purpose eventually produce less and less benefit. Diminishing returns is also known as *marginal utility* or *marginal productivity*. In graphic form, this axiom resembles an S leaning toward its right side; hence, the designation "lazy S curve."

## INVESTMENT RETURNS

The amount of benefit produced by a given investment. Investments are made with the expectation that the return will equal or exceed the amount of the investment by at least the prevailing interest rate. When applied to budgeting, *investment returns* suggests that the benefits of any given expenditure, if they can be monetized, must equal or exceed that expenditure by an amount derived from the application of an appropriate interest rate to that expenditure. Assuming an expenditure of $100,000 and an interest rate of 5 percent, the benefit must total at least $105,000 for this expenditure to be admitted to a budget as an appropriation. This benefit level of 105 percent is also known as an *admissibility criterion,* which represents a hurdle, or threshold, for proposed appropriations.

## LAZY S CURVE

See *Diminishing Returns.*

## LINE-ITEM BUDGET (LIB)

A budget featuring things to be purchased. By relating appropriations to commodities, line-item budgets represent a "shopping-list" approach to allocation problems. This approach is believed to express official and citizen interest in the values of economy and control. Also known as *traditional budgeting.*

## MARGINAL PRODUCTIVITY

Axiom of economic thought which suggests that any given investment does not produce the same amount of output as the preceding increment. Therefore, every expenditure aggregation passes a point, known as "the margin," where further additions produce increasing output, but at a decreasing rate. See *Diminishing Returns.*

## MEASURE OF EFFECTIVENESS (MOE)
Refers to the degree of goal attainment. Statements of effectiveness are frequently expressed in terms of proportions. For example, if a school has a goal of eventually graduating 95 percent of its tenth-grade class and it achieves this goal, the school can be deemed 100 percent effective.

## MEASURE OF PERFORMANCE (MOP)
Refers to production indicators such as demands for service, work loads, numbers participating, and test scores. Without measures of performance, one cannot derive unit measures, the fundamental concept of performance budgeting.

## OTHER SERVICES AND CHARGES
Object classification which covers all those expenses that cannot be classified as personal services, supplies, or capital outlay. As a residual category, it includes such expenses as professional services, telephone charges, advertising, printing, and rent.

## PERFORMANCE BUDGET (PerB)
A budget which relates appropriations to work loads. By featuring unit measures, performance budgets are believed to express official and citizen interest in the managerial value of efficiency.

## PERSONAL SERVICES
Object classification which identifies expenses for salaries, wages, and other forms of employee compensation, such as sick leave, pension contributions, and insurance premiums.

## PLANNING/PROGRAMMING/BUDGETING SYSTEM (PPBS)
A budget which relates appropriations to goals by means of benefit calculations. By striving to integrate planning, programming, and budgeting activities, budgetmakers seek an investment pattern based on the analysis of alternatives.

## PROGRAM BUDGET (ProB)
A budget which relates appropriations to goals. Budgetmakers practicing this approach strive to appropriate sums to nonorganization, goal-oriented cost centers. Program budgeting is believed to express official and citizen interest in planning and in the effective use of resources.

### SUPPLIES
Object classification which embraces such commodities as stationery, operating materials, expenses for repair parts, and maintenance supplies.

### UNIT COSTS
A unit measure derived by dividing investments by measures of performance.

### UNIT MEASURES
Unit costs, units-per-cost, and unit times.

### UNITS-PER-COST
A unit measure derived by dividing measures of performance by investments, usually expressed as units per $1, per $100, or per $1,000.

### UNIT TIMES
A unit measure derived by dividing staff hours by measures of performance. Unit times are useful because they do not reflect currency inflation and they focus attention on the relationship of technology to production.

### ZERO-BASE BUDGET (ZBB)
A budget that relates appropriations to priorities. Budgetmakers using zero-base budgeting try to focus on the future by establishing an ordinal ranking for all expenditure proposals, independent of historical experience and comparisons.